Maxyne Gaelynn Bursky

GOOD DOGS

with

BAD NAMES

A playful and purposeful journey through the world
of breed rescue, with tips on how to adopt
the dog of your dreams!

i

GOOD DOGS with BAD NAMES
And Other Purebred Rescue Adventures

by Maxyne Gaelynn Bursky

www.GoodDogsBadNames.com

ISBN: 0-9821555-0-6

Dedicated to Richie, my soulmate,
who has always found room for one more

*Special thanks to Carol Ackroyd, Toby Affron, Aron Bursky,
Christine Davis, Judith Ditfurth, Patricia and Edwin Hamilton,
Patrick and Lisa Mansell, Ken and Kathi McClure, Denise Moore,
Mike and Dawn Sereg, Christina Soto, and Donna Subramanian for
their help, patience, and unwavering encouragement*

For Bupkis, Yankel, Jello, and Lucy

Hey, I just heard your human call you "Rover." That isn't really your name, is it?

"Rover" is the name she gave me. But she mostly just calls me "What-Did-You-Do."

Table of Contents I

Table of Contents II
Some *Really* Good Dogs

1

The Shout Test

Years ago, I adopted a Boxer/Bulldog mix in a moment of weakness. I say weakness because I already had both a pack of eight dogs and an absolute, bottom-line, don't-even-think-of-it ultimatum from my husband, Richie, that there is no more room at the doggie inn. Fortunately, Richie is a closet pushover. He says no but always means yes!

This little female had been tied to a tree in the backyard of a house. Three weeks before, the occupants had moved out. This dog had nothing but a pail with green, slimy water and a dish of insect-covered kibble to sustain her. She had begun howling, and thankfully, some neighborhood children climbed the fence and brought her to their home. The parents phoned a friend who, luckily, happened to be president of **St. Bernard Rescue**. They hoped that Robin would be able to place the dog, or know of a group who could.

Within the hour, Robin was parking her Saintmobile in front of the kind family's home. Once she safely tucked the dog into a soft crate in the back of her SUV, Robin phoned me to see if I could take this baby. Her belief was, the best chance of placement would lie with a group specializing in at least one of the breeds this dog resembled, and I was (and still am) with **Buddies thru Bullies English Bulldog Rescue (BTB)**.

The minute I set eyes on this sad creature, I was toast. That miserable little body, ribs sticking out, and giant "I'm coming home with you, right?" brown eyes were too much for my nonexistent backbone. I took her home and hid her in the bedroom until I had crafted a verbal profile of her that Richie would be unable to resist. It worked like a charm.

I thought it would be adorable to name her "Bupkis," the Yiddish word for "nothing," since she was hardly a whisper more than that on the first day I saw her. Well, the name seemed like a good idea at the time.

"Bupkis" rapidly began to gain both weight and confidence. I soon discovered she loved to dart out the front door. I thought we were doing pretty well with her "down" and "stay" training designed to get her used to being in one of those positions when the door opened. Not that fateful Tuesday night.

It had been a pretty hectic day for me. It wasn't until 10 p.m. that I realized I had forgotten to take in the day's mail. Unthinkingly, I thrust open the front door to retrieve my bills from the mailbox, and "Bupkis" grabbed the opportunity to dash out.

She streaked down the middle of the street like her butt was on fire. I was in hot pursuit, all the while screaming, "BUPKIS! BUPKIS! BUPKIS!" Some of the homeowners way down at the other end of the road clustered together, gaping at the lunatic woman clad in red and white striped socks, shoeless (I didn't have time), sweatpants, and giant white T-shirt (my leisure uniform) flapping in the breeze. Just think how many votes for the straitjacket I received that night as I flew through the neighborhood yelling what I once thought was a clever dog name at the top of my lungs.

Word to the wise: Test out the name you have chosen before conferring it on your dog. Go out in the backyard and scream it to the high heavens. Don't worry about violating the noise ordinance in your town. If shouting that potential name seems to create an aura of insanity, go with your instinct. That name choice will create a reputation ("There goes that weird neighbor who named her pooch 'Dammit'") that will "dog" you as long as you live there. So give pause for the paws. (I did catch up to "Bupkis" eventually.)

After consulting many breed dog rescue volunteers both in person and online from my own group as well as others, I have compiled not only the tired, worn-out labels we stick on our hapless pets, but also some wonderful, creative names. My mission in giving "Dear Labby" advice is to share my Yoda-like wisdom so that the entire dog-loving world may benefit.. One major jewel of knowledge is

3

this: Be careful what you name your dog; you never know when you will find yourself screaming that name at 10 o'clock at night while sprinting through your neighborhood.

One further example of naming one's dog while simultaneously experiencing a brain fart comes to me from an otherwise sensible acquaintance. She frequently congratulated herself on her wittiness when she conferred the title of "Hay Yoo" on her gorgeous Collie.

Alas, one day "Hay Yoo" set out on an impromptu and unauthorized tour of the local sights. Her owner followed at a frantic pace, yelling the dog's name in unrestrained fashion. Needless to say, in the process of recovering the Collie pup, several people watching the doggie drama unfold responded in a wide range of interesting ways to the sound of "HAY YOO!" hurled in their direction.

2

A Dog By Any Other Name Would Smell As Sweet

When a breed rescue accepts a surrender dog that has the same name as another dog already in our care, we don't change their name, but add a number. This numerical labeling continues from January through December of a particular year, and then we go back to zero again on New Year's Day. "Winston" (conjuring up images of the great British leader, Sir Winston Churchill) is, to put it mildly, rampantly popular with the English Bulldog set. By last September, we were up to "Winston 6." Another popular name for this stocky, muscular package of stubborn fun is "Tank".

Imagine this: An invisible dog-naming fairy-sprite has perched on your shoulder as you gaze transfixed at your newly acquired Samoyed. Just as the words, "Let's name him 'Snowball'" are about to fall from your lips, that unseen spirit screams into your ear all sorts of horrible noises that distract you and thus prevent you from making such an awful mistake.

In your startled state, you hear angels singing. You're driven to call your dog something as special as he is. Suddenly, your command of the obvious fades and, miracle of miracles, out of your mouth pops the name "Chantal" or "T-Bone."

Begone, "Fifi" for Poodles (although, I must admit, it might work on a Rottweiler for a touch of irony). Farewell, "Blackie" for *any* dog of that color. Goodbye, "Jack" or "Russell" for a Jack Russell. Consulting the "experts," I have taken the most common names for each of the breeds featured herein and listed them in a sort of avoidance guidebook for new dog moms and dads.

Some of you may spot a name in the "forbidden" pile that you have always wanted to name your dog. I say, go for it anyway. You may already have "Fido" nuzzling you in your lap. I say, don't worry, be happy. Naming your Collie "Lassie" is hardly a sin; in fact, it probably ranks up there with secretly eating a dozen jelly doughnuts at midnight while dieting. All I ask is when presented with a naming opportunity, you think your way past the common names to find a great one for your new companion.

If you adopt or acquire a dog that already comes with an undesirable name, fear not. Once you get "Fido," you can rename him. The easiest way is to initially continue calling him "Fido," and sprinkling your interactions with high-energy bursts of "CODY! GOOD BOY!" Before long, that dog will

6

ecstatically respond to the more positively reinforced shouts of "Cody," and forget all about the "Fido" debacle of his past.

In this book, I have listed several breed rescues and their websites under each grouping of what I and other "experts" agree are common or obvious names. Pay them a cyber-visit and note the frequency with which certain names come up either specific to that breed or across the board. "Max" and "Princess" are among the monikers that plague nearly every canine group. After searching through a dozen sites, the common denominators will rear their ugly heads to mock your secret love of the name "Benjy." You'll see.

BASSET HOUND

PAWS DOWN

Lucy	Snoopy
Stretch	Cleo
Daisy	Beauregard
Stumpy	Shorty

PAWS UP

Liberty	Hammy
Zayna	Trudy
Eudora	Elwood
Belinda	Enchanting

Laurabelle

Collette

www.TristateBassets.org
www.NewEnglandBassetHoundRescue.org
www.bhrg.org

CHIHUAHUA

PAWS DOWN		PAWS UP	
Tiny	Chi-Chi	Bambam	Smoochie
Jose	Pedro	Destiny	Tea Rose
Pepe	Precious	Ipod	T-Bone
Taco	Peanut	Houdini	Lolly

Wally

Monte

www.ChihuahuaRescue.com
www.AZChihuahuaRescue.org
www.Chihuahua-Rescue.com

3

What Were They Thinking?

Animals from a pet store, puppy mill, "backyard breeder" or even well-respected breeder that are discussed in this book are no longer living with their original owners. These beautiful babies ended up as wards of rescue for a myriad of reasons, including but not limited to one or more of the following:

- ☹ **We're moving and can't take the dog.** (Would you leave your child behind?)
- ☹ **I (or one of my family) is allergic.** (Then get a hypoallergenic breed like a Poodle or Portugese Water Dog and stop whining!)
- ☹ **The dog is too big for us now.** (This is especially ridiculous when the breed surrendered is an English Mastiff or Great Dane. Question to original owners: When your three-month-old puppy weighed 60 pounds, did you think that was the top of the growth chart for him?)

- ☹ **The dog barks too much.** (This is a favorite of **Beagle Rescue,** lovers of the dog bred to bark when it sees something worth paying attention to.)
- ☹ **We have a new baby.** (Then it must be time to throw the *dog* out with the bathwater.)
- ☹ **The dog that we already have doesn't like our new puppy.** A subset of this is: The dog we have had for the last 10 years is too old to keep up with our new puppy. (So the old guy gets the boot.)
- ☹ **The dog keeps (a) peeing in the house, (b) digging in the yard, (c) eating the couch, (d) all of the above.** (Dogs can be trained.)
- ☹ **We're getting a divorce and neither of us wants the dog.** (This is a sad, sad case.)
- ☹ **My ex gave my kid a Christmas present of this dog. I can't take care of it and my kid always forgets about it.** (This is a good reason why many shelters are careful about adopting out during holidays.)
- ☹ **I got this dog from a friend who got it from a friend and it's driving me crazy.**
- ☹ **It costs too much to feed.**
- ☹ **I can't afford (or don't want to pay) the vet bills.**
- ☹ **My apartment complex doesn't allow dogs this size, but I thought I could get away with it.** A variation of this nonsense is: My apartment complex doesn't allow dogs, but I thought I could hide it.

☹ **I couldn't bear to bring the dog to a shelter, so I left it in a field.**(Now classified as a stray by the pound who retrieved it from the field two weeks later, the dog is too emaciated to be put up for adoption.)

The air of frustration surrounding this list comes from the knowledge that a lack of education about dogs spikes the numbers of pets surrendered to both shelters and private rescues every year. Each person that calls our hotline with one or more of the issues above always receives a few suggestions designed to prevent breaking the established bond between the dog and its humans. After all, there are sometimes teary-eyed children (and adults) hoping for an alternative to sending the dog away, and we are almost always overflowing with intakes.

The happy ending we seek here is that a family has remained intact. They consult a trainer skilled in behavior modification, and the dog is behaving beautifully. People on a tight budget are directed to county-run clinics if available. The apartment dweller pays a damage deposit and the landlord allows the animal to stay. Each species under the roof understands the other's needs, and everyone is now living in harmony. Relieved, everyone happily piles into the minivan and rides off into the sunset. These are, unfortunately, more the exception than the rule.

That being said, we now turn to the potential of a happy restart for those dogs who missed out on the minivan/sunset deal. In the final example in bold above, which is one of the worst-case scenarios, the now weakened pooch is whisked away from the pound in the SUV of a breed rescue volunteer who will deposit him with his foster family and begin his journey through rehab to his forever home.

Every rescue group in this nation, whether they take in all pets or specialize, will tell you that the worst time of the year for them is January and February. The ranks of the unwanted usually swell to proportions unmatched during the rest of the year as the novelty of the animal given as a holiday present wears off. Summertime is a sad runnerup to Christmas, as brainless families dump their pets rather than pay for kennel care during vacation. These surrenders are often heartworm-positive, since it is likely their dummy owners have skimped on vet care.

The surrendering post-Christmas human is often a distraught single mom steeling herself to be The Grinch. Her ex-husband has cleverly bought his kids' affection by surprising them with a dog or cat on December 25th. Meanwhile, Mom is working two jobs, has no time to spend with The Gift, and two months after The Giving of The Gift, the kids are either too young or too busy to feed or walk it. The dirty job falls to Mom to separate her offspring from what should have been a stuffed animal under the tree. She now has many little tears to dry, and we now have a bewildered pup to rehome.

If that dog or cat came from a government shelter and is being returned to the same facility, that never bodes well for the animal. Many municipal shelters have a policy that a pet that comes back to them is deemed to be unfit for adoption, sort of the two-time loser effect. Euthanasia is usually the next step.

It's important to find out in advance if the place you are returning an unwanted dog or cat is what is termed a "No Kill" shelter. If they accept him, they will hold on to him until he is adopted. That, of course, is a double-edged sword, since that severely limits the amount of space available for intake there.

Breed rescues never euthanize their fosters to make room for new ones. In fact, for just about all breed rescues, the only time the decision is made to put dogs down is when they are suffering from a painful medical condition from which they will surely not recover, or if the dog is too aggressive to be placed. In either case, no matter how justified this final act of love for the animal may be, it is at great emotional expense to the volunteers. And it never gets easier to make this decision, whether for the rescuer, veterinary staff, or owner.

In nearly every breed adoption agreement, there is a provision which insists that if the adopters ever decide to surrender their dog, that family must bring her back to the breed rescue. Don't even think about going to the pound with her. We do not want the dog going into a government system from which she may

15

never return. Many breed rescues have taken to microchipping, a process whereby a minuscule sort of computer-coded ID tag is painlessly inserted between the shoulders of the dog. The code, once scanned, reveals the name of the owner and facilitates getting the animal returned home.

To ensure one of their adopted dogs does not end its days in a shelter after adoption, a rescue group may register the microchipped foster dog in the name of the organization itself. When a shelter scans that chip, it notifies the breed group that one of their dogs is there. Now the pooch is back under the rescue's protection.

If the dog actually went missing and its owner is searching for it, they are joyously reunited. If the dog was dumped at the shelter, the adoption contract is null and void. Game over. The pup is again set up with a foster family until a different adoption can be arranged.

There are countless times when a call goes out for last-minute short-term foster families to accommodate the incoming for two or three days until we can settle the dogs somewhere more permanent. That's when the volunteer stress level hits the roof. Dogs are not the only ones who learn to sit up and beg; foster committee members looking to recruit new volunteers are well-trained to perform that trick.

In the examples above where the rules of a landlord are being violated, or where the dog ends up in the hands of someone who took him in on short notice as a kind gesture and now regrets it, there is often no other option than surrender.

All of the reasons, stories and excuses used for surrendering a pet demonstrate why an extensive adoption application and home interview are essential before a rescue deems a family worthy to take home one of their boarders. Anyone who rents their home must produce a note on landlord stationery accompanying their application. The note must specifically state that a dog of the size and type applied for is acceptable to live on the premises. Additionally, if you already have other pets at home, a letter on your vet's stationery must attest to the health of your menagerie, that all vaccinations have been given, and heartworm preventative purchased.

The majority of online rescue groups have a fairly detailed rundown on their websites of what to expect financially if you want to take on a dog of that breed. The site of **Southern States Mastiff Rescue** clearly states, "Are you prepared to spend $250 a month in the care of your dog?" An English Mastiff, at an average of 175 to 200 pounds, is among the gentle giants that require larger quantities of food than other breeds. The vet bills are often higher because a large dog who is ill gets a greater volume of meds than the average Yorkie. Yet Yorkies and Lhasa Apsos require frequent grooming, which may swell the budget. Too often, when passing a pet store, people seduced by the cuteness in the window don't stop to think what it will take to keep that ill-bred but adorable puppy in good shape. Suffice it to say that anyone who calls to surrender a dog and is adamant about giving her up, no matter the reason or excuse, that person will be accommodated to the best of our ability. That is not to say that we believe the owner's story necessarily, but if we have any feeling that the dog could otherwise end up in a kill shelter, or simply be released on the street, that pup is definitely coming home with us, no (dog) bones about it!

4

We Never Met a Dog We Didn't Like

Upon receiving a call from a kennel that a Bulldog in their care had not been picked up by his owners for several weeks past the pickup date, I drove over to take the legally abandoned dog. "Samson" was a gorgeous example of his breed, tan and white, with broad shoulders and narrow hips. He was friendly but quite weak, and a sickly sweet odor filled the air of my car.

When I arrived at the vet's office, "Samson" was diagnosed with parvovirus, and it was determined that he was beyond help. As we prepared to end his suffering, Anne, a tech who had worked there for years, came in to the examining room to assist. I decided to remain during the process. After all, in this short time, I was his only friend.

What touched me deeply were the tears streaming down Anne's

face as we held "Samson." She had met him only seconds before, and was already grieving for him. "It never gets easier," she sobbed. Yet once "Samson" had gently slipped away, Anne glided to the next examining room with a big welcome for a perky Shih-Tzu and its owner, and she continued the day.

All over the country, privately established full-breed rescues labor to save dogs. There are rescue committees attached to many show-level dog clubs, and they will carefully scrutinize homes for dogs surrendered to them. Many breed rescue groups are unaffiliated with these clubs; yet both are dedicated to rehoming purebreds.

The independents, as it were, consider it their mission to remove injured, sick and abandoned purebred dogs from city and county shelters that rarely have the funds or the room or the expertise to rehabilitate a less-than-healthy animal. The pounds have their hands full as it is with the avalanche of vigorous pets that come into their care.

Private groups also take animals from puppy mills, where it is likely that the critters have spent their lives crammed in cages, unsocialized, and often rife with hereditary ailments. These volunteers nevertheless stand ready with enthusiasm, hope and optimism when the four-legged prisoners are liberated.

In the past, many government-run facilities would be forced to euthanize all those pets needing serious TLC. But with the advent of these stand-alone grassroots breed rescue organizations, scores of furry bundles of love have been saved and eventually united with their forever families.

The techs and administrative people at city and county shelters are the lifeline for abused or injured purebred dogs. Without their cooperation, we would never know of the existence of the dogs relegated to sick bay or the back room kennels, the ones the public won't see.

Dianna, an employee of a Middle Georgia animal shelter, emailed me with a dilemma that only a private rescue could solve. A severe cruelty case had just come to a close in her jurisdiction. Thankfully, the offender was not only fined but also jailed for his heinous acts. Justice like this is rarely meted out for animal abuse, and the slimebags often get away with hardly more than a slap on the wrist.

Among the dogs and other animals that had been found starving in this man's apartment was a people-friendly but reportedly dog-aggressive English Bulldog. Dianna and her staff were initially free of the normally brief time limit set for caring for the surviving pets, as the county police department designated the animals as evidence, to be maintained until the outcome of the trial.

Once that trial was over, however, the "evidence" was no longer needed, and the pets were demoted. That meant that shelter workers had just a week to find permanent homes for those dogs and cats before they would be euthanized. Dianna insisted that I come get "Archie" the Bulldog immediately. I am certain that dozens of pets have been saved by her getting on the stick and mobilizing breed rescues to come down ASAP and pull those animals whose time was nearly up.

When I picked "Archie" up, he appeared well-fed and happy. He had a few fleas, but nothing major. He had had all his shots and was neutered. Our vet performed the necessary tests and pronounced him heartworm-free.

After a refreshing bath outside my home, smelling of lavender, "Archie" was slowly and cautiously introduced to the members of my personal pack. Although tentative at first, he got along wonderfully with everyone, male and female alike. It is my belief that all those months cooped up in a kennel made him socially awkward and self-protective when he got around other dogs. He seemed thrilled to finally be free.

About a month later, a great family from Virginia traveled down to meet him, and it was love at first sight for everyone. Shortly after, I received a delightful photo of "Archie" lounging on the living room couch with his new brother, a Pug named "Bullwrinkle."

Although they are formed and run by private citizens, each breed rescue group in this book, as are dozens of others, is a federally recognized charity to which legitimately tax-deductible contributions may be made. If you are searching through the hundreds of breed rescues on the internet and want to be sure they are a group recognized by Uncle Sam, check to see that they have posted their 501(c)(3) designation. That's the magic title.

Understand, however, that not all rescue groups, especially the very small ones new to the scene, have the time or the manpower (or even sometimes the awareness) to go through the massive paperwork required to secure the 501(c)(3). This does not necessarily mean that the group is not committed to saving lives. If you find yourself interested in working with or adopting from a rescue like this, you need to do your research and check them out.

Also understand that only the dollars that you contribute to the support of a 501(c)(3) group are recognized as tax-deductible. Claiming a writeoff for your generous contributions to those other organizations, appreciated as they are, just won't fly at audit time. Nevertheless, our furry friends can't (or don't) want to read IRS documents, and animals don't care who saves them!

DACHSHUND

PAWS DOWN		PAWS UP	
Weiner	Weinie	Cameo	Piper
Doxie	Snoopy	Slinky	Damian
Oscar	Sausage	Dweezle	Cayenne
Hot Dog	Slinky	Quigley	Nona

Butch

Ernie

www.mwdr.org
www.AlmostHomeRescue.org
www.DareToRescue.com

DALMATIAN

PAWS DOWN		PAWS UP	
Spot	Domino	Skittles	Darby
Sparky	Oreo	Noelle	Echo
Perdy	Pongo	Tonka	Athena
Dot(tie)	Dally	Fletcher	Toby

Mike

Dozer

www.AdoptASpotDalRescue.com

www.DalmatianRescue.com

www.SecondChancesDalRescue.com

5

Helter-Skelter, No More Shelter

Every day, the decision is made to euthanize animals because they need more care than a municipal facility is equipped to offer. When the pound staff determines that a German Shepherd, for instance, is too ill or beat up or emaciated to be put up for adoption in the short window they have available, the visionary shelter will call or email the local **German Shepherd Rescue** (and by "local," the rescue headquarters could be a hundred miles or more away). If the breed group responds immediately and commits to picking up the dog, they will have as few as 24 hours or as much as a week to retrieve him.

The person within the Shepherd organization who has received the message relays it to the group's members who are closest to the municipal shelter, and under **GSR's** authorization, transports the dog either directly to a rescue committee member experienced in assessing initial intakes, or some miles down the road to the next transporter. Step by step, the rescue railroad volunteers get the dog to its first foster stop. These canine convoys are comprised of people willing to drop whatever they're doing to jump into the car and burn rubber to get one more animal out of harm's way.

The internet has been an absolute godsend for rescue. In addition to all the chat rooms that have sprung up dealing strictly with specific breeds, there are also cyber meetup groups for dog fanciers. There you can post thoughts and opinions on hundreds of topics of interest particular to your pooch of choice.

Offering your email address to the rescue group you associate with means that from time to time you will receive an appeal for help in different ways, including taking a leg of a trip between municipal shelter and foster home for a new dog; volunteering to represent your group at a dog event or even at one of the large pet supply chains like PetSmart or Petco; or financially sponsoring a particularly needy dog already in rescue who is amassing a wad of vet bills.

In addition to being a **BTB** executive board member, I am on the email list of several rescues in my area, including **Southeast Bloodhound Rescue (SEBR)**. When a mass email calls for volunteers to transport a hound from Tennessee to Georgia, for example, the trip is divided up by the group's director into stretches of 100 miles or less, and all comers are invited to participate. Within days, **SEBR's** coordination will have that Bloodhound safe and sound in its new digs.

It is not unusual for me to agree to drive one or two legs of a rescue road trip with a German Shorthaired Pointer in tow, only to hand him off at the end of my portion of the journey to volunteers from **Great Dane Rescue,** who will tote the pup to the point where people affiliated with **Boston Terrier Rescue** carry him to his destination.

In years past, the telephone was the only means to put a project like this together, and it took many more hours to put a traveling lifeline on the road. Because the internet allows the process to be streamlined, a greater number of animals can be saved.

6

What You Don't Know Can Hurt Them

Each breed has specific medical issues more common to that type of dog than any other, and those issues are often magnified as the dog's popularity increases. More backyard breeders try to squeeze out some fast cash at their home by mating purebred dogs of questionable genetic health and indiscriminately selling their puppies to anyone with greenbacks. For example, one of the conditions that plagues the Shetland Sheepdog (Sheltie), among others, is thyroid malfunction, a problem exacerbated by poorly informed, unqualified people breeding to make a quick buck.

Well-respected breeders will endeavor to have their breeding adults and/or puppies tested for discernible common problems, and present the future owners with proof of health and guarantees before even allowing the pups to leave the grounds. A caring, professional breeder will insist that you become familiar with the specific personality traits that can emerge (why they were bred to look and act a certain way). The breed rescue will point out what to expect from your dog, especially for the first-time dog owner.

When a particular breed of dog comes into rescue, life circumstances such as possible previous abuse can result in aggression in various forms. For example, a dog who has been starved or maltreated in other ways may threaten other animals or people by growling protectively over his food bowl. Some dogs, having been abused by a man, may distrust men in general.

Dogs not properly exercised or allowed to relieve themselves at appropriate intervals may have difficulty with housebreaking. Thankfully, with the help of trainers and experienced volunteers, most of the negative issues weighing down these victims can be reversed, or at the least modified, to make them the good canine citizens they need to be.

When a shelter dog with unknown background comes to my home or to the home of another first-line volunteer, he is given a thorough bath (sometimes two) and all those annoying little hitchhikers (fleas and ticks), which sometimes number in the hundreds, are removed. At times, the toenails are so long that they have curled up under their pads and made it difficult and painful for the dog to walk. If the pup is cooperative, he gets a major pedicure; if he hates his feet worked on (as is occasionally the case), to the groomer he will go.

I suspect that the casual observer watching the new arrival consume his first meal in rescue would consider the scene a comical one. I am accustomed to taking a rubber arm, with attached hand, and carefully and slowly sticking it into the food bowl while the dog is eating. If he ignores this intrusion, it's a preliminary indication to us that a child coming up to "Rover" and fooling with the kibble is not going to be in any danger.

Toy possessiveness can also be a factor. When that ball is in the new dog's mouth during our playtime, the first time I attempt to retrieve it, I wear a padded glove to minimize any chomping damage that might result if the game goes sour. It's a primitive way to determine how much behavioral modification the new addition needs to go through. I am grateful that the kibble and toy tests usually come out favorably with our rescues.

The fact that breed rescuers know the general attributes of the dogs in their care is such a plus for people seeking a purebred pooch to call their own. Those looking for a family protector, for example, would do better with an Akita than a Great Dane. (I must admit, however, I have met some mushy, laid-back Akitas who just did not get that memo.) It is an easy mistake to misinterpret the look or size of a dog as an indicator of dominance or the lack thereof. Too many people end up with a pet they are dissatisfied with, through no fault of the animal. Unfortunately, the result could be a one-way trip to the pound.

Through the use of detailed adoption applications, home visits and informative orientation sessions, breed rescues have had tremendous success placing their charges into permanent homes. Using information posted on their websites, conducting telephone and home interviews, these groups attempt to outline all possible issues or misconceptions the public has traditionally had about their breed. The rafters may be full of Dalmatians in foster care, but **Second Chances Dalmatian Rescue** will gladly and gently decline to offer one of their dogs to an individual or family unprepared to care for a pet requiring tons of activity.

If streaks of drool on the walls of one's abode is not acceptable, for heaven's sake, don't get a St. Bernard! My own Saint was so talented that he managed to lob a few hunks of saliva 20 feet in the air, and my vaulted dining room ceiling was quite a work of art. Researching the characteristics of one's dream dog can save everyone, including the dog, a lot of heartache.

A wonderful and wildly successful fundraiser in which I participated when I lived in Florida is the **Broward County Humane Society's** Walk for the Animals. Back in 1993, I took "Zeesa," my Pet-Aided Therapy Great Dane, on the Walk. With her jet-black coat and flashy white paws, the 175-pound girl cut quite an imposing figure. As is typical with Danes, she was a docile creature, and was the sweetest, largest, hairiest throw pillow a couch could ever accommodate.

While "Zeesa" and I waited for the Walk to begin, an awestruck dad rushed up to me with his three-year-old daughter. She had never seen a dog that big, and she was fascinated. After a few minutes of pup and tot getting acquainted, the man attempted to hoist the little girl up on to "Zeesa's" back, explaining that he wanted to take a picture of this phenomenon as a souvenir of the day.

Almost instinctively, I lurched to keep the toddler from alighting on my dog, four hands now holding the child while her legs dangled in midair over the unsuspecting pooch. I gently reassured the gentleman that he didn't have a snowball's chance in hell of getting a photo of his child astride SuperDog. These gentle giants have delicate backs, I explained, and just can not sustain a physical burden like that. He was actually very understanding and at the same time surprised to hear this information. I suggested that the next time he wanted a pony ride for his kid, he should find a pony.

Not 10 minutes later, when a Sun-Sentinel newspaper photographer asked if I would mind putting "Zeesa" in a sit/stay while he positioned another willing dog owner's miniscule Yorkshire Terrier, I could not refuse. The Yorkie's head was barely bigger than "Zeesa's" paw.

Both dog moms looked on proudly, knowing that these guys were going to be newspaper celebs by tomorrow. I imagined "Zeesa" putting her autographic pawprint to scores of copies of the pending photo for distribution to family and friends.

That just wasn't in the cards. The three-pound hound craned back her tiny neck to get a glimpse of the creature she was partnering with in this venture. "Zeesa" politely responded by lowering her head and touching noses. Mistake. Big mistake. A growl that sounded more like the motor of a toy car erupted from the throat of the furry shrimp, and pandemonium ensued.

My Monster Terminator Canine of Ferocity frantically backed away from the little terror, knocking over, domino-style, a bunch of Basset Hound Club members. I lunged for "Zeesa's" leash to prevent her from continuing in reverse. My hopes for fame and fortune were dashed. No amount of coaxing could get her near that Yorkie again. In fact, "Zeesa" stayed nervous for a good half hour, eyes darting from side to side in case "Attila" (not her real name, I hope) was waiting in ambush.

It was certainly crystal clear to everyone within 20 yards of this scene who the four-footed wimp was. The lesson to be learned from Terrier University is that no matter how small they are, Terriers can not only be sweet, cuddly companions, but also feisty and a force to be reckoned with. Of course, every breed has its own special appeal. It is vitally important, though, for people to be as educated as possible about the general characteristics and particular needs of their dream dog.

7

My Dog's Better than Your Dog

I once had the good fortune of manning a table at a pet exposition sponsored by the local county animal control. Under several canvas pavilions were a bunch of rescue groups, and each table was covered with brochures for education, glass fishbowls inviting contributions, and various items for sale, often breed-specific, such as mugs or T-shirts with the pet of choice emblazoned on them.

That year, a bunch of shirts had been donated for us to sell at the expo featuring the image of a gorgeous, super-wrinkled English Bulldog with the caption (shamelessly stolen from the National Dairy Council), "Got Bulldogs?" It's my eminent opinion that people who adore a particular breed will buy anything within their budget (and sometimes outside of it) that has that breed's image on it. I am obnoxiously proud of the curio cabinet in my home that houses what my husband calls The Shrine. It is filled with ceramic, plush and porcelain variations of Bulldogs.

Some years ago, a wonderful, small-budget film hit the big screen entitled *Best in Show.* It was a loosely-scripted comedy that spoofed the dog show circuit. Most all rescuers are familiar with this little gem. For a good portion of the movie, I laughed at the characters in all their supercilious glory. Then came a scene where two of the principal people, owners of an adorable Norwich Terrier named "Winky," were being interviewed in their home.

Lo and behold, every inch of their living room was filled with NT knickknacks, statues, lamps and blankets. My merriment toned down a bit as I sat in the dark theater. I realized I was looking at a reflection of myself and of many other chumps who gasp in delight as they see their favorite breed sculpted in clay and begging to be bought. The dream of owning an actual dog of that breed? Priceless. For everything else, there are credit cards...

Sitting next to me at the pet expo was the proud president of **Golden Retriever Rescue**. He had brought a photo album filled with pictures from their past year's Retriever-attended events. Most notable were the photographs of their annual picnic which had taken place only a month before. One frame in particular held the fabulous image of 55 (no joke) Goldens under a grand shade tree, all reclining casually, without their people. The dogs were calmly relaxing, a wonderful island of blond fur, while their owners were somewhere outside of the frame of the picture.

I gasped in admiration, commenting that Bulldogs had such a wide variety of dog-to-dog personalities, that the maximum number of leashless bullies in our summer picnic photo would probably be two. Or one. And the owners would not be more than a few feet away!

Many among the bull breeds like to be the only dog in the family. When there are Bulldog-attended events, like our annual Bullympics festival, 50 to 60 Bulldogs and their human entourages show up. The bullies registered for the annual shindig proceed to knock over or plow through the obstacle course in the most absurd and enjoyable way, and a great time is had by all. Every owner, however, is instructed that their precious champions must remain on leash and attached to their persons except when performing feats of athletic prowess. (Reality check: the "balance beam" is a foot wide and an inch off the ground, and still the participants fall off.)

A few years ago, I attended a picnic hosted by **St. Bernard Rescue** in South Florida. Of course, there were tons of beautiful Saints lounging in the shade of the park pavilion, and friends associated with other rescue groups dropped by to share in the fun. A large, musclebound, middle-aged man with three hulking Newfoundlands ambled up to the refreshment pavilion. In speaking to him, I learned that Newfies and Saints were astonishingly popular in this subtropical state. He commented that one of the biggest problems **Newfie Rescue** had was educating people to keep these beautiful animals indoors. So many of the types of dogs bred for northern climates suffer and die from heat exhaustion in the warmer states. It is imperative that their potential owners are aware of this, as well as the initial steps to take in case a dog begins to show symptoms of collapse.

At the same picnic, a lady who runs **Chihuahua Rescue** in the area decided to avail herself of a few hot dogs and a soda. She had a bit of a rough time, however, because of the way she was dressed. Since Chi's are so much easier to transport than, say, Irish Wolfhounds, this rescuer decided she would bring a bunch of dogs to the party in a novel way.

How convenient that she had two baby backpacks at home, the soft cloth kind of pouch a young mother can sling over her back to carry the baby close to her body. The Chihuahua lady had hung one carrier across her chest, and one against her back, and filled them with no less than six yapping little darlings. I was reminded of the creature from Greek mythology, the Gorgon Medusa, with its coif of hissing snakes.

What amazed me was how feisty these 5-pound bundles were! It was as if this lady had put on a bullet-proof vest made out of furballs. Chatting with her over the din of these barkers, I discovered what most 'little dog' owners know, and that is, these are BIG dogs in tiny dog suits. They are sweeties, without a doubt, yet they are also typically territorial, protective and dominant. You can be sure if there were any sort of a pickpocket in this woman's vicinity, the crook would do well to look elsewhere for a victim rather than chance an encounter with these guard doggettes.

These exchanges with the Golden Retriever president, the Newfie man and the Chihuahua lady typify the inherent knowledge that each rescue has of their breed. This breed know-how inures to the benefit of each and every applicant who is looking to add a canine member to the family. There are people who want the personality and attributes of a totally laid-back, giant Newfoundland; some who dream of a calmly playful Golden Retriever; some who are looking for a scrappy Chihuahua; and some who long for the tough-looking but gentle-mannered English Bulldog. The breed rescuer is the person to let you know whether theirs is truly the kind of dog you are looking for.

DOBERMAN PINSCHER

PAWS DOWN		PAWS UP	
Dobie	Diablo	Peyton	Autumn
Rambo	Dutchess	Bravo	Skye
Duke	Caesar	Scorpio	Slater
Sam	Raven	Isis	Gracie

Kahlua

Samantha

www.dru.org

www.DobieRescue.org

www.ILDobeRescue.com

ENGLISH BULLDOG

PAWS DOWN		PAWS UP	
Winston	Tank	Charlotte	Elvira
Dozer	Butch	Bonehead	Fancie
Rocky	Wrinkles	Mister	Punkin
Buster	Lucy	Jolie	Sweet Pea

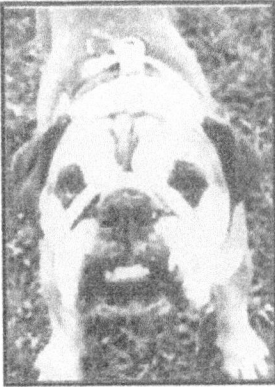

Handsome

Yanker

www.HeavenSentBulldogRescue.org

www.BuddiesThruBullies.org

www.EBullyMatch.com

8

Okay, Where's the Hidden Camera?

It's always an adventure to answer the phone or respond to an inquiry about adoption or surrender. Just when I'm ready to greet the world with a smug, know-it-all, heard-it-all smile on my face, the cellphone sings, *Who Let the Dogs Out?* and I'm on my way again, humbly rounding out the learning curve. Education, whether it be about animal care, choosing names, or nuclear fission, is always the preferred path over ignorance; yet sometimes I think I would rather be left in the dark. The bottom line is, there are some questions that are better left unasked, because the answers, I fear, beg to be preceded by, "Are you *really* that stupid?"

I had been deeply involved with rescue about two years when I heard the gravelly voice of a man, maybe 50-ish, on the other end of the phone. The conversation went something like this:

"Do you fix your male Bulldogs?" he asked.

"Yes," I replied rather self-righteously. "We neuter and spay all our dogs before we release them for adoption."

A big pause. "When I get my dog, can you make sure to save his testicles in a jar in case I want to reattach them for mating later on?"

I simply wrapped up the conversation with a quick "NO" and looked around the room to attempt to discover the hidden cameras. Some 25-year-old wearing a wildly patterned silk shirt with palm trees on it and holding a microphone in his hands would surely burst from the clothes closet any minute with the war cry of, "You've been punked!"

Another, shall we say, ballsy comment found its way to my ear when a woman inquired about the advantages of neutering. I pointed out that testicular cancer was one of the things she would not have to worry about for a neutered male dog.

Her next question skeptically asked, "Well, what percentage of neutered dogs die from that kind of cancer?"

With all the restraint I could muster, I politely answered, "Zero."

"That's impossible," she declared. "You have a lot of nerve making false claims like that. You can't cure cancer."

"Lady," I said, "there ain't no balls cancer where there ain't no balls."

One more pathetic conversation needs to make its way into this chapter. It's more scary than stupid, in my view, and points up the absolutely predatory nature of those determined to create and maintain puppy mills. A friendly, soft-spoken young man called to "reserve three bitches and two stud dogs" before they were fixed. Well, I just had to poke the snake.

"Why do you want to adopt so many dogs?" I asked brightly, the little hairs beginning to stand up on the back of my neck.

"We've always loved Bulldogs, and we know how much you can get for the puppies. So my wife and I thought it would be a great idea to start a breeding farm."

I choked back the intense desire to choose words that would embarrass a sailor, and blandly asked his name and where he hailed from. With that vital information secured, I launched into a lecture so hellfire and brimstone about the sins he was on the brink of committing against the animal world that I knew I would bring him to his knees, begging forgiveness. Too bad he hung up on me five seconds into my glorious sermon.

Armed with his name and location, however, I immediately fired up my computer and hit every rescue group I knew of asking them to pass on the info, in case Bulldogs weren't the only animal of choice for these nuts. I assumed that they would refine their inquiry since it had not met with a favorable response, and I wanted to ensure as best I could that they wouldn't get their hands on even a hairball, let alone a living, breathing creature. My return emails from rescue groups all reflected the same sentiment.

When speaking with legitimate potential adoptive folks, I assure them that there is no dumb question to ask about the care, treatment or temperament of the dog or the dog breed that they want to take home. But as with all aspects of life, there are those who push the envelope so far that it just doesn't pay to look for a stamp.

9

(Breed) Rescue Me!

Breed rescues are essential in the overall scheme of rehoming dogs. The role of the **Humane Society** and its branches across the country as well as the **Association for the Prevention of Cruelty to Animals (ASPCA)** and other such pillars of animal protection is essential to not only saving the lives of pets generally, but also promoting legislation that affects the welfare of millions of animals at a clip. Where the grassroots private breed rescues excel is in the personal attention to the smaller numbers of dogs. The breed rescue volunteer knows her foster dogs' attributes and foibles intimately, and can communicate this knowledge to potential adopters.

While the vast majority of individual breed rescues are relatively small, placing anywhere from 5 to 100 dogs per year in new homes, there are some breeds who have tightly organized, national networks responsible for the saving of hundreds of dogs per year. Many Greyhound, Dalmatian and St. Bernard rescues, to name a few, work under a national framework. This setup can make it easy for the person searching for one of those dogs to adopt in his or her area by going on these websites and clicking the state they live in. There are breed rescues that are able to use the power of their numbers and pool their funds, so that one chapter needing a little extra money for an expensive hip dysplasia operation, for example, can apply for a distribution from the national.

There are many people who visit our website and zero in on a dog whose picture graces the site along with a brief synopsis of how he came to us, what his temperament is, and what medical issues he has, if any. Sometimes an online visitor downloads the adoption application and mails it in with a note that targets a particular dog. "I am interested in 'Rosie,'" the note could say, "the three-year-old brindle female you have on the website. I have always wanted a brindle."

In the preliminary phone interview, the volunteer might tell the expectant dog mom or dad that although they might want a brindle bulldog – brindle being a pattern of coloring that resembles tiger striping – "Rosie" would not be right for them, since the family has twin toddlers and a baby, and "Rosie" has demonstrated strong toy possessiveness. Even though "Rosie" is doing well with her behavior modification training, there is no way that a rescuer will place a dog with that sort of issue in a home with small children. "Rosie" will find her happy home with a retired couple, a family with teens, or a person living alone. And the family with the brood of little humanoids will be presented with a choice among the more gentle fosters, albeit a different color than requested. They could also be given the option of waiting for a brindle Bullie that would fit their lifestyle, but who had not yet become available.

"I have always wanted a Dalmatian because the puppies are just so cute!" Substitute any dog breed into that sentence, and watch that breed's rescue personnel start to shudder. Most likely, whoever utters those words is doing so after looking at greeting cards with that dog's likeness in adorable poses; after seeing a movie where the dog star performs what seem to be miraculous feats of havoc and/or heroism ("Lassie! Get help!"); or from just deciding, without knowing anything about the behavioral traits or maintenance needs, that that look and shape makes a statement about the owner. Strap a spiked collar onto a beautiful, muscular Rottweiler, and you don't need to wear a T-shirt that says Tough Guy. It's the image that counts.

Breed rescuers love to discourage people who they feel are a mismatch from adopting a particular type of dog. Way too many people will buy a puppy from a pet store or through a classified ad on impulse. The puppy is so cute, or popularized by the media, or has a reputation as a fearsome watchdog. Out pops the credit card in the pet store, or cash to the neighborhood pseudo-breeder, and the new owners take home an animal, with no clue as to what appropriate care or training is necessary.

As a **BTB** volunteer, I have frequent contact with well-meaning individuals who buy a Bulldog because they love that massively wrinkled face and stocky build. Unfortunately, the contact is most often when they are surrendering their dog, now out of the puppy stage, because it was too expensive to keep going to the vet for the various and sundry issues that can beset this breed. Educating oneself about the type of dog you want is the first step in a successful meld between two- and four-legged family members, and preventive maintenance is an essential lesson to learn.

A close friend of mine, a now-retired veterinarian (may *all* veterinarians and vet techs be sainted), spent many hours treating dogs from breed rescues at vastly reduced fees. She once jokingly remarked that when she would see a client in the waiting room with a Shar-Pei puppy, she would begin to plan what part of her home she would be remodeling that year. It was her experience that a good number of visits to the vet could be avoided if the pet owner did a once-a-week "tuneup" on his dog. This regular attention to the physical needs of your pet, which can mean different routines with different breeds, will keep you out of the doctor's office by eliminating minor problems before they develop into major ones.

Don't be afraid to ask your rescue to be specific about the sort of maintenance their breed requires. You stand to enjoy a long and debt-free relationship with both your vet and your furry companion.

GREAT DANE

PAWS DOWN

Scooby-Do	Goliath
Thor	Zeus
Harley	Apollo
Patches	Tiny

PAWS UP

DaVinci	Diamond
Mr.	Twink
Pickles	Romeo
Stella	Tony

Braun

Max 5

www.GreatDaneRescueInc.com

www.RMGreatDane.org

www.GreatDaneRescue.org

53

GERMAN SHEPHERD

PAWS DOWN		PAWS UP	
Max	Shep	Talia	Dakota
Rin-Tin-Tin	King	Cinnamon	Lucas
Rex	Princess	Tootsie	Courage
Prince	Sarge	Hocus	Pocus

Lucas

Rosie

www.gsrnc.org

www.GSDRescue1.org

www.magsr.org

10

Buddy, Can You Spare a Dime?

Every rescue group has a board consisting of volunteers who take on various leadership roles in saving the dogs. There is fundraising, fostering, interviewing, and the list goes on. Officers are given standard titles like president, VP, and secretary-treasurer. Nevertheless, it's often the case that whatever mantle you wear will not cover all the duties you will perform, and most volunteer leaders in breed rescue don several hats.

I am hardly the only one in **Buddies thru Bullies** who accepts rescue applications, does phone interviews, home visits, transport, fostering, fundraising and public relations, often juggling several of these jobs simultaneously. These labors of love are performed while working full-time, raising a family, and attending to those other pesky details of living, not the least of which is tending to one's own dog pack. In my home, that consists of four mellow charmers: two English Bulldogs, an English Bulldog/American Bulldog mix, and a Boston Terrier. And let us not forget, of course, the occasional foster Bullie.

Aside from the Bullympics which I mentioned before, we have one other major fundraiser which allows our 400 member families to participate even though they are spread out over nearly 40 states. We lovingly call it the Zero-K Run. It was aptly named to honor the English Bulldog's tendency to take cabs around the yard rather than bothering to expend any energy on the useless running routine enjoyed by other dogs.

We encourage members to take photos of their dogs dressed in running gear and send them in to be published in our quarterly newsletter, *The Bullytin.* Depending on the size of the donations collected by each member to "sponsor" the armchair athlete, various graduating prize packages are awarded. The top prize has been a four-foot by four-foot Bulldog plush that appears to be an absolute necessity for some families. The majority of the rewards, donated by various companies, include dog nutrition suppliers, pet toy manufacturers, and Bulldog-themed T-shirt creators.

The beauty of the event is that there is very little overhead, so everything we collect goes straight to the dogs. Although I would love to claim that this no-show concept is originally mine, there are variations that other rescues utilize. One group has an annual Don't Come Picnic. Invitations are sent out instructing each guest to send in $20 to *not go* to a specified park on a specified day for the un-event. One also has the option of paying $40 to ensure being *un*invited to the following year's picnic. There is even a refreshment committee set up! Volunteers are asked to choose from a variety of tasks and supplies ordinarily needed. Each item carries a price tag, and checks are sent in for fantasy hot dogs, napkins, trash bags, etc. The UnRun, as we have nicknamed the Zero-K, is also marvelously successful.

The adoption fee charged by a breed rescue generally includes a year's membership in its group. There is often a monthly or quarterly newsletter featuring information on upcoming activities, articles recognizing contributions, and announcements of recent adoptions. Participation in local celebrations hosted by your rescue allows you to meet like-minded lovers of that breed. These gatherings are a blast, and it's a great opportunity for the dogs to socialize with their own kind. It is exhilarating to see a big bunch of beautiful Siberian Huskies making eachother's acquaintance. It's like a convention, only without the name tags and funny hats.

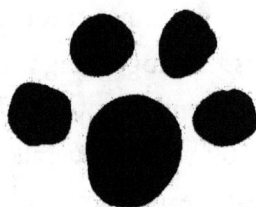

11

Is There a "Sucker" Sign on My Back?

Each of my dogs has his own story how he came to be a Bursky family member, but "PT," my Bulldog mix, has a really special one. In 2004, a bunch of hurricanes hit South Florida back to back, devastating many areas. Residents of mobile home parks are especially vulnerable during hurricane season, and there were news accounts of major destruction in many of those neighborhoods.

Along with the property damage and the potential for human injury comes the large-scale abandonment of pets. In the face of an impending hurricane, flood or other natural disaster, I am sure I speak for every pet rescuer on the planet when I declare that I will NOT go to an emergency shelter unless my dogs can come too. Local civil aid departments are coming to realize that many people will not leave their pets behind, and changes in the "no animals allowed" policy are slowly being made. Nevertheless, it is unlikely that my husband and I would be welcomed in the local high school gymnasium toting four or more dogs. So I'll stay put and hope the roof doesn't blow off.

Immediately before and after the hurricanes of 2004, dogs and cats were being dumped at Animal Control facilities in droves, and the frantic workers had little choice but to put them down nearly as soon as they came in the door. "Overcrowded" was a miserable understatement describing the shelters at that time, and calls went out over whatever means from the techs to any and all private rescue groups who could make it there.

One such call was received by Toby, the **BTB** rescue committee chairman. A kind employee at the **Belvedere Animal Control** shelter north of West Palm Beach had contacted her, desperate to have her come up and claim two English Bulldogs who had been left there just before Hurricane Charley hit. The word "no" is rarely in the volunteer's rescue vocabulary, so off she went.

When Toby arrived there, the employee informed her that in addition to the two purebred Bulldogs, there was a handsome, gentle Bulldog mix who was slated for euthanasia within a few hours if not spoken for. With over 20 foster dogs already in our care at the time, and the two new ones promising to stretch our resources to the limit , Toby begged the worker not to bring out the mix and to just please produce the EBs. The shelter tech agreed, and went in the back to gather up the two purebreds.

Within minutes, the worker reappeared with three dogs in tow. Toby fell in love with my future "PT" immediately. With a few friendly epithets hurled at the tech for her caring but blatant manipulation, Toby loaded the two English Bulldogs and my mutt into her Toyota Corolla for the trip back.

Not to be outdone by the pound's vet tech, my buddy invited me up to see the new rescues she had gotten from Belvedere. This has always been a practice of hers, to get feedback from other board members on a dog's demeanor or suggestions for which family would make the best foster placement or adoption. So I didn't suspect a thing. But once I got to Toby's place, the first dog I was introduced to was the beautiful mix who (*sniff sniff*) was saved from certain death and now desperately needed a home.

As if on cue, "PT" rolled his giant baby browns and locked eyes with me. I was a goner. After that, no amount of practical haranguing from my husband could sway me from piling "PT" into the Burskymobile and transporting him to his forever home at my address. Toby had played me like a violin, and there was one less casualty of the pet population disposal system.

"PT" is a great addition to my family. As I write this, he is training to be a Pet-Aided Therapy (PAT) dog. His gentle nature makes him perfect for visits to hospital-bound children and seniors in nursing homes. I am especially proud that "PT" will be joining the ranks of the many dogs saved from euthanasia who make a big difference in special people's lives.

61

12

The Pay Is Lousy but the Benefits are Great

One of the key words recurring in the dog adoption scene is VOLUNTEER. I am talking about the noun, as in, "I am a *volunteer*, so if you send in an application to adopt on Monday, and you don't hear from me by Friday, don't assume that I am incompetent, inefficient, or just plain lazy." I would personally love to be drowning in applications so that our rehabbed beauties are virtually flying out the foster families' doors and into the arms of their adoptive family packs. At the same time, there are only so many hours in the day to devote to my passion, and occasionally I conduct a preliminary interview and phone orientation weeks instead of days after receipt of completed paperwork.

As I mentioned, Toby is responsible, along with a rotation of helpers, for the majority of our fosters, so when she decides to go out of town for a week, the executive board sprouts a new bunch of grey hair. It is difficult enough finding care for a dog or two when one set of foster parents goes on vacation. Ensuring that 15 to 20 dogs in various stages of rehab are being appropriately nurtured, along with supervising some very part-time but dedicated volunteers, is a next-to-impossible task.

As the beads of sweat began to collectively form on our brows, the **Buddies thru Bullies** board furiously conferenced how to solve this dilemma. Out went emails appealing to the membership to step up for whatever amount of time they could put toward the bullies' care. Within a day of the posting, our public relations coordinator, Lisa, and her husband Matt offered to fly from their home in St. Louis to Florida and spend *their* vacation time caring for the bunch. They used some frequent flyer miles for part of the airfare and put up their own funds for the remainder of the expenses.

There is nothing like spending your hard-earned free time scooping up mounds of poop, dishing out tons of kibble, and then later, scooping up mounds of poop. A cruise in the Caribbean pales in comparison.

Upon hearing of the couple's generosity, other **BTB** members sent checks in to cover their expenses. The pair were not out of pocket for a penny. This is the volunteer machine working at its best. To my constant delight and amazement, this is not an isolated instance of rescue group members opening their hearts and their wallets when aid is most wanted and needed.

Lisa and Matt are surely the volunteer's volunteers, but rescuers who read this know that a story like this is not unusual. The battle cry remains, "It's about the dogs." Just do what needs to be done.

A lick from just one of those pink tongues makes it all worthwhile.

13

We're No Pushovers

BTB is not alone in the procedures we follow to secure the perfect family for the perfect dog. When we first receive an application, we conduct a phone interview based on what information was submitted. We let the applicant know all the potentially unpleasant things our breed may cause an owner to experience, medically, behaviorally, etc. Understand, though, that "unpleasant" to someone unfamiliar with a breed may not necessarily be "unpleasant" to us rescue loonies. For example, all of my dogs snore like they're sucking the walls of the house in and back out again; but I am not disturbed by it, and consider it quite entertaining at times. I will admit, though, there are a few in my extended family who do not share these sentiments.

Recently, a 26-year-old single man was bent on getting himself a Bulldog. Never having had one before, he happily took home one of our beauties, a brindle and white 10-year-old surrender named "Freckles". Mario had had his telephone orientation, a home visit, and was primed for bullie ownership. The one drawback which the volunteer had pointed out to him was that "Freckles" slept as if she were surgically attached to a bullhorn. Her snoring was at the top of the charts. And this bright, kind young man lived in a studio apartment. There would be nowhere to hide from the nighttime decibel level.

"No problem!" Mario grandly reassured us.

Needless to say, "Freckles" returned to us after two weeks of her would-be owner earnestly searching for noise reduction aids. He padded her crate. He bought earplugs. He even tried a white noise machine to drown out the dog's nocturnal serenade. Alas, all efforts were in vain. Saddened as he was, we suggested Mario check out a few other breed rescues whose canine candidates wouldn't be quite as loud after sundown.

*   *   *

So many people are unaware that even the most expensive breed of dog can be directly adopted from a breed rescue, and at vastly reduced cost. Because these organizations are small and privately run, they are fiercely dedicated to saving one particular type of canine (although some of them do occasionally take in other breeds, or dogs whose appearance indicates that they are probably mixed with the type to which the group has devoted its efforts).

Yes, the initial cost of bringing a purebred rescue dog into your home is vastly less than the dollars needed for the purchase of a puppy from a responsible breeder, or a pet store (heaven forbid). Note the words "initial cost." The range of fee for adoption from my group runs anywhere from $50 to $450, with the most often quoted price running between $200 to $250. The price tag for a Bulldog puppy can be between $1,000 and $3,000. Going through breed rescue will mean significant initial savings.

There are several subtle factors that play into the money side of the adoption issue. Rarely are puppies surrendered to breed rescue organizations, unless they are either the sickly product of a puppy mill or a youngster is so ill that the original owners do not want to shell out the thousands it may take to fix him. The bill can be daunting for palate surgery, ligament repair, treatment for severe allergies, heartworm or demodectic mange. And the list goes on.

In the case of a severely ill puppy, we take care of his medical issues the best we can through our affiliated vets, and adopt him out to a member of our group experienced in what will likely be either a long and arduous recuperation, or a chronic condition requiring above-average attention. So when an applicant requests a puppy, it will be quickly explained that that is a rarity.

We usually suggest the adopter instead set his sights on a lively adult. Dogs ranging from two to eleven years of age have all sorts of energy levels, from the two-year-old couch potato who insists that you have a limo available to take him around the yard, to the eleven-year-old lunatic who throws himself against the car windows as you roll up to the dog park, eager to make new friends.

There are always a few seniors available. Almost without exception, a rescue website will sport a small text block appealing for potential adopters of elderly dogs. Frequently, the reason for surrendering an aged dog is that he doesn't get along with a new, younger dog, and the older one is the loser. We often refer to senior surrenders as permanent fosters. They will live out their lives in the corner of a room on a soft pet bed, watching the parade of other dogs entering the foster home and later leaving upon adoption approval.

The comment most often made to the interviewing volunteer when a family declines to consider a senior is that there is not enough "life mileage" left on them to sustain a long-term relationship. Ironically, the temperaments of these elder statesmen are overwhelmingly ideal for young children who want to just curl up with a gentle, quiet creature who requires minimal maintenance, yet offers tons of affection.

GOLDEN RETRIEVER

PAWS DOWN

Goldie	Maggie
Jake	Bailey
Murphy	Clancy
Sam	Buddy

PAWS UP

Chomper	Violet
Summer	Haley
Karat	Haven
Lainie	London

Conner

Diamond

www.grrcc.com

www.grra.com

www.grreat.org

GREYHOUND

PAWS DOWN		PAWS UP	
Grey	Speedy	Blair	Malachi
Dasher	Chase	Chantal	Kilauea
Racer	Lightning	Lorelei	Maizie
Bus Boy	Streak	Opie	Jonah

Finn

Zeph

www.GreyhounDog.org

www.GoldenGreyhounds.com

www.GreyhoundRescueRehab.org

14

I Can See Clearly Now, The Money's Gone

The cost to adopt a dog is inversely proportional to the cost of his rehabilitation. A dog that comes in as a stray to a municipal shelter, and that is mercifully released to a private rescue group, may have multiple problems to be dealt with before he is ready to be presented to his forever family. The most frequent condition is malnutrition, followed by a positive indication for heartworm disease, open sores from dog attacks, and so on. The majority of dogs coming in to shelters are not neutered or spayed, and it is often the responsibility of the private group, depending on the agreement with the shelter, to assure that no more puppies are born of those who come home with rescue.

Don't for one minute let the lower cost of a breed rescue dog fool you into thinking that the adoption price is an even exchange for the expenses of keeping that dog in rescue. A rescue committee will often charge a family $300 for an animal whose vet bills total more than $3,600. Every rescue club is more than familiar with the red ink that flows from doing what it takes to make a dog medically and sometimes emotionally whole again.

The cost to the rescue group may also be many times higher than the agreed-upon adoption fee simply because the adopter faces, for example, having to spend $40 a month in prescription eyedrops for a dog with a condition known as dry eye; occasional x-rays updating the vet and owner as to how their pooch is faring after his anterior cruciate ligament (knee) operation; or the advance of arthritis and need for meds and special treatment for a senior dog. Utilizing creatively packaged fundraisers, charity events, grants from private foundations, and good old unsolicited donations, rescues attempt to make up the shortfall. In addition, veterinary ophthalmologists, orthopedists, dermatologists and other specialists toss thousands of dollars of fees to the wind in order to give these orphans the same top-notch treatment a Westminster champion would receive.

What is paramount is that we find those perfect, loving environments in which a dog of a particular breed and temperament will be happiest. But we also want to make the initial cost attractive and affordable to loving families who could not otherwise afford the price tag for their favorite breed.

Rescue groups work very hard to cultivate relationships with great veterinarians, many of whom are knowledgeable about the particular breed whose treatment they would subsidize. Visitors to our website often request the name of a Bulldog vet in their area. The doctor angels who work with rescue not only charge reduced fees for our foster dogs, they have even donated their services completely free when a special needs dog comes into our care with overwhelmingly expensive but manageable medical conditions.

Some years ago, an English Bulldog came to us with multiple problems, one of them being severe dry eye to the point that he could barely see. Even medicated drops were not helping. "Buster" had skin allergies as well, but his foster mom (eventually his adoptive mom), Andrea, wouldn't give up on him. She cooked for him, used herbal remedies, and his coat filled out beautifully; but his eyes remained critically uncooperative. Even our ophthalmic veterinarians were running out of options.

A member of our group, studying at the University of Florida to be a veterinary technician, cajoled her doctor buddies at the school to take a look at "Buster". After numerous tests, it was decided that "Buster" would have an unusual and expensive operation, with all of the UF medical personnel who were involved donating their time and ample talents.

"Buster's" condition was caused by his tear ducts refusing to produce enough moisture to protect his eyes. I know the veterinarians will forgive me for oversimplying the procedure, but these miracle workers created a pathway from his salivary glands to his eyes. Once the bandages were removed and

"Buster" was pronounced as having achieved maximum medical improvement, his peepers were awash in tears – well, saliva. For months, the joke in our circle was that every time "Buster" looked at a meatball, he would start crying!

Not all fees for tests and procedures can be waived. Even our vets and techs have to pay the rent. But when we run up our accounts at animal hospitals – and we surely run 'em up – there is rarely a prod from their offices to pay down the balance. Their unending patience while awaiting our sporadic payments has saved countless lives. We never have to worry that a dog will go untreated if our pockets are empty. Upon receiving a long-awaited grant or collecting monies from a major fundraiser, it's tremendously satisfying to be able to cut checks to our medical supporters that bring us to zero balance with them. Of course, they all know that next week, that palate surgery or pneumonia treatment is going to thrust us right back into the red zone.

To help with costs, the following is a direct suggestion to rescue groups nationwide (if you're not doing this already). One of our rescue workers came up with a fantastic idea that helps us with feeding upwards of 20 dogs at a time and keeping costs down. It is a very creative, win-win scenario.

Many of the large pet supply chains and feed stores around the country are more than willing to donate the bags of dog food which are set to expire by the end of a month. All the rescue group has to do is secure permission from the store manager to enter the store at the time that is designated for the bags' removal and start loading up the shopping carts.

FYI: It helps to have a business card, and a formal request on rescue club stationery when you first talk to the store manager. That will go a long way in the credibility department. Then he or she will not suspect that you are simply looking to get free food for your own dogs by masquerading as a rescue group. Casually mentioning that it can also save the store employees' time when you remove the unsalable merchandise wouldn't hurt either.

If one branch of a superstore rejects the idea, don't be discouraged. Each individual store may have its own policies, so charge ahead to the next branch. Also, be aware that some dog food companies will, to some extent, reimburse retail outlets for expired product, and those brands will, of course, be off-limits. After all, the stores are in business to make money. If they have the opportunity to receive a refund of sorts from kibble producers, the stores will choose that option. But there is still plenty of dog food left to make establishing a food-removal program worthwhile.

The true lifeblood of breed rescue is the rank-and-file members of these groups. These are the families (individuals who have adopted from us are considered families as well) who, after paying their fee to take home a new four-footed dependent, and after the complimentary year of newsletters and invitations to meetup events, continue to pay dues to support the organization. These are people from all walks of life, all financial levels, and all parts of the country who share one common theme: love of that particular breed. It is not unusual for a group's treasurer to receive a greater sum for membership renewal than the one specified on the annual bill.

Each and every family who adopts from a breed rescue group is a living, breathing advertisement for that group. Of vital importance is the awareness this family creates for their friends, neighbors, for strangers in a pet-friendly store, at a dog park: that breed rescue is a great option for would-be pet owners. A happy, mannerly example of a rescued purebred out and about is the best recommendation for making the choice to rehome a dog rather than buy a puppy.

15

Where There's a Will...

If I were to create a diagram to show how the human world makes the greatest difference in the lives of creatures who cannot speak for themselves, I would first draw a series of concentric circles. At the center, of course, are the dogs. The next layer would consist of the boards and committees of all the rescue groups who effect dramatic changes in those dogs' lives. Surrounding and supporting them are the dues-paying members of each organization, including adoptive and foster families. The outermost category is composed of the Good Samaritans. They just seem to appear out of nowhere when the need arises, perform miracles, and blend back into the general public.

I've been awed time and again by the giving spirit of so many individuals who step up to help and are not always directly connected with the rescue process. They are simply interested in making a difference.

The year 2003 saw two three-legged dogs enter our rescue sphere in the same month. The male had been missing a limb since birth. "Daisy Mae," the female, had been disabled after she tangled with a lawn mower and the mower won.

Brenda, a longtime volunteer, had an idea which involved an acquaintance of hers, owner of a local prosthetics lab in Plantation, Florida. Brenda called me a few days after her lightbulb moment, explaining breathlessly that this specialist had enthusiastically offered his services to create an artificial leg for "Daisy Mae." The lab had never before crafted a limb for a dog, but that didn't stop them. The staff saw the project as an exciting challenge.

In four short weeks, "Daisy Mae" was outfitted with a sturdy new gam. Fears that she might have difficulty adjusting to her support evaporated immediately as "Daisy Mae" trotted confidently across Brenda's living room on the very first try!

This prosthetist was not in the least interested in adopting a Bulldog, nor any dog, for that matter. He simply wanted to help. His skill and hands-on commitment to make this dog whole again is a perfect example of one person's simple commitment to make this world a better place. I'm so grateful for that lab's special contribution. Sometimes people show up in our lives just when they are needed most.

I must take a moment here to look in the mirror and offer

congratulations to a seasoned rescuer for being able to finally exert self-control when it comes to the fostering process. I no longer attempt to keep every dog that comes into my care while it waits for the perfect adoptive family. There was a time that the only family I could envision as appropriate for my drooly boarders would be my own, and the number of my canine children climbed, as I mentioned before, to as high as nine.

I am not alone in this tendency. In fact, my numbers pale in comparison to some incredible individuals who run private rescue programs. At times, even rescuers of giant breeds are accustomed to fostering 200-pound beauties numbering into the teens. It was amazing to go into the home of Robin and Glen, dedicated **St. Bernard Rescue** volunteers, and see a few of these magnificent dogs in each bedroom, relaxing in unimagined comfort and security!

Fortunately, for my husband's sanity, I have since learned that there are tons of wonderful, caring people in the world who are just as capable of love and devotion to their adopted dogs as any rescuer; and I have happily surrendered to the reality that the snoring of five critters in my home (the four dogs and my hubby), plus an occasional foster pup, is perfectly adequate. There are many rescue volunteers who happily release their well-adjusted, four-footed guests to approved applicants.

There are many selfless people in these groups who are my personal heroes, because they are the ones who rush to the shelters to claim a dog for rehab who they know will always be the last in line to be chosen by a family. These are the dogs missing limbs, like "Daisy Mae"; the blind ones; the deaf ones; the ones with coats scarred by neglect, or worse; the ones who have given up on trusting a human. To the untrained eye, these dogs are the unsalvageable, the deformed, the rejects, the losers. Look closer.

The three-legged Irish Setter who leaps over couches; the blind Labrador who hears the clink of the cookie jar opening and gets to the kitchen faster than his sighted littermate; the deaf Dalmatian who springs into action when his owner uses the hand signal for GO; the 14-year-old Boston Terrier who plays like a puppy; the Brittany Spaniel who winces out of fear when a hand is raised only to pat his head; I will take any one of these dogs over the privileged progeny of a Best In Show winner.

The true heart of rescue lies with the people who scoop up the dog with the tired eyes and despondent demeanor; who cradle the animal in their arms and murmur lovingly to it; who joyfully declare him to be their own permanent foster – a totally transparent euphemism for, "He's mine!" The mantra of rescue is, "No dog, damaged in spirit or body, gets turned away."

Certainly, there are always practical considerations that can create obstacles to fulfilling that credo, with money, space and time topping the list. I have sat and cried with other rescuers when it was clear that we could not respond to a family who wanted to surrender their dog. There wasn't an inch of space available anywhere; the foster families were full up and there was simply no room at the inn. The up side in that scenario is that in about half of surrender cases, the dogs are still residing with their families, albeit the ones who want to give them up, and the people are willing to hold on to their pets until other adoptions from the group free up the rescue welcome wagon.

With the expansion of breed rescue programs, dogs in record numbers are being placed into private foster care, leading to eventual adoption. More animals than ever before are being neutered and spayed. The deadly scourge of pet overpopulation is losing its potency every day.

16

Yes, We Have No Bananas (or Cats)

There are a couple of items I would like you to keep in the back of your mind, the most important of which is that this book is *not* about cats. I fully admit that I am completely in the dark about cats and cat rescue. That being said, please be sure that, wherever I praise and, let's face it, gush about the virtues and selflessness of my dog rescue buddies, you mentally add in cat rescue people. I know cat rescuers have a hard row to hoe, with the feline population exploding not only on the domestic front, but among outside-living (feral) cats.

I have always marveled at those people who will put out food and water for wild, feral cats. These animals, to my limited understanding, barely allow a person to handle them; yet there they are on the back porch or the side of the house, fully expecting a meal and fresh water – and getting it. My hat is off to people who put out humane cat cages to capture these untamed felines, get them neutered and vaccinated, and then tenderly release them back into the "wilderness".

This is truly unconditional love. No purring furball in your lap to deliver comfort and satisfaction in the traditional way; the reward is simply the knowledge that those yowlers in the back yard or living in the woods will have a better and healthier life, and will not reproduce in numbers that spell starvation for so many kittens.

I grew up in a household where my mother was terrified of cats. There was no traumatic event leading up to this phobia; she simply froze in fear at the thought of any feline coming within miles of her. Hence, I was deprived of getting to know a cat or kitten in any intimate way during my formative years.

When I reached adulthood, I began volunteering at my local **Humane Society**. I specifically asked to be assigned to the cattery. I figured that, now that I was on my own, and Mom was nowhere in sight, I would get up close and personal with a whole new universe of pets.

The best experience I had in the cat compound was actually while cleaning their cages. I had reached "Tabitha's" quarters. She was a big, beautiful orange and white tabby. After giving her fresh food, water, and shredded newspaper, I replaced her in her little dorm. But this girl was not finished with me.

As I turned my back to her closed cage, preparing the refreshments for the next kitty, "Tabitha" shot her long, flashy paw through the bars on her cage door and grabbed on to the back of my shirt. Her claws managed to grasp the hooks of my bra. In a snap (so to speak), "Tabitha" opened my upper undergarment right through the shirt! There was an awkward moment when I realized that that upper-body freedom I was experiencing was cat-caused.

Before making the appropriate adjustments to my intimate attire, I carefully backed up to dislodge her claws from my shirt. I was just inches away from the cat, and I wanted to avoid hyperextending her already outstretched paw.

When I moved back in her direction, "Tabitha" apparently took this little mambo as a signal that I approved her action and she readied to up the ante. Out shot front paw number two, and my back was covered with affectionate, gentle grabbing, pummeling and pulling.

All this activity had not gone unnoticed by my fellow volunteers, and within what seemed to be merely seconds, the cattery was filled with hysterical laughter (I think even the other cats were amused). Not one of the other volunteers was in the least sympathetic to my dilemma. Only after dozens of jokes at my expense did someone separate cat and bra and allow me to jiggle my way to the restroom for the needed fix.

Although I am focused on dogs and dog rescue, I do appreciate the contribution that cats make to our lives, and my frayed underwear is a testament to that contribution.

*   *   *

Like thousands of other web surfers, I am addicted to what written cyber-goodies are offered in my daily "in" box. One of the funniest messages I have received to date was from my best friend of 40-plus years, Denise Moore. Throughout her life, Denise (a/k/a Dee) and her daughters Amanda (a/k/a Pooh) and Elizabeth (a/k/a Boomer), have endeavored to save and/or adopt both dogs and cats of every conceivable variety.

Denise is one of those special people who will stop her vehicle in the middle of the road, block traffic, and, oblivious to the danger, get out and pick up the bony little kitten or puppy making its way across the busy boulevard. She then takes it home and hands it what I like to call the keys to the kingdom: a soft pillow in the kitchen, a trip to her beloved vet, and what seems like all the food and toys a PetSmart can sell.

One day Denise sent me an email piece entitled *How to Give a Cat a Pill*. She had found it somewhere on the internet shortly after wrestling to medicate her present cat, "Freddie," a/k/a "Fast Freddie," a/k/a "Fast Flatulating Freddie".

This is something many cat owners will appreciate. It gave me a tiny, tongue-in-cheek look into what all it takes to care for a feline. It sure ain't just buying a few cans of Fancy Feast and a rubber mouse.

By the way, the following little warning is for those of you who watch new car commercials on TV and ignore the itty-bitty disclaimer that often appears at the bottom of the screen, *Professional driver on closed course: DO NOT TRY THIS AT HOME*. With that caveat, read on:

How to Give a Cat a Pill

"1. Pick cat up and cradle it in the crook of your left arm as if holding a baby. Position right forefinger and thumb on either side of cat's mouth. Gently apply pressure to cheeks while holding pill in right hand. As cat opens mouth, pop pill into mouth. Allow cat to close mouth and swallow.

"2. Retrieve pill from floor and cat from behind sofa. Cradle cat in left arm and repeat process.

"3. Retrieve cat from bedroom and throw soggy pill away.

"4. Take new pill from foil wrap, cradle cat in left arm, holding paws tightly with left hand. Force jaws open and push pill to back of mouth with right forefinger. Hold mouth shut for a count of ten.

"5. Retrieve pill from goldfish bowl and cat from top of wardrobe unit. Call spouse in from yard.

"6. Kneel on floor with cat wedged firmly between knees. Hold front and rear paws. Ignore low growls emitted by cat. Have partner hold head firmly with one hand while forcing

89

wooden ruler into cat's mouth. Drop pill down ruler and vigorously rub cat's throat.

"7. Retrieve cat from curtain rail. Get another pill from foil wrap. Make note to buy new ruler and repair curtains. Carefully sweep shattered figurines and vases from hearth and set to one side for gluing later.

"8. Wrap cat in large towel and get spouse to lie on cat with cat's head just visible from below armpit. Put pill in end of drinking straw. Force mouth open with pencil and blow down drinking straw.

"9. Check label to make sure pill is not harmful to humans. Drink one beer to take taste away. Apply bandage to spouse's forearm and remove blood from carpet with cold water and soap."

And on up the disaster scale it goes. The last line of the piece speaks to me personally: "How to Pill a Dog: Wrap pill in bacon, cheese or peanut butter. Make him beg." Although I have run across a persnickety pooch or two, that's right on. Dog pilling time is rarely a clash of the titans.

*　　*　　*

There are tons of privately established mixed-breed dog rescues throughout the country. In addition, many breed rescues will take on a dog, space permitting, that is a combination of their specific breed with another, since there is the potential of finding him a home with a family open to adopting a "distant cousin," if you will. There are also animal rescues that take in dogs, cats, ferrets, pigs, horses; if they need a home, these groups are there to help.

In this book, I am focusing on what I know best, and that is my experience with breed rescue. Yet I will not ignore the powerful and selfless contribution that mixed-breed groups, in fact, that advocates for animals of all kinds make in creating a better place for the domestic animal population in our society.

JACK RUSSELL TERRIER

PAWS DOWN		PAWS UP	
Jack(ie)	Russ	Rugby	Kirby
Eddie	Dammit	Bopper	Kimmie
Milo	Wishbone	Windy	Starlight
JR	Scrappy	Toonie	Rainbow

Freddie

Lola

www.RussellRescue.com

www.RussellRefuge.org

ST. BERNARD

Fred and Ginger

www.SaintRescue.org

www.AllSaintsRescue.com

www.COSaintRescue.com

17

Do Your Homework

If there is a breed that you have thought about owning, before you buy a brand spanking new puppy, consider the following:

☻ Go on to the rescue websites. Unsure of how to access them? At your search engine, type in phrases like "dog rescue" or "Boxer rescue," whatever breed suits you.

☻ Make your choice. Take the time to visit the web pages of several rescues that focus on the dog you like, or think you like, and look at the dogs available for adoption; read their stories.

☻ Click on the FAQs (frequently asked questions) and learn what it takes to bring one of these great creatures into your family. Note: if you don't have a computer, or don't know how to navigate your way around the web, ask a friend or co-worker to get you where you need to be and then print out the information. A cyber-geek is never too far away.

☻ If you are in the same local area as your chosen group, think about being a foster family. Not only can you familiarize yourself with the breed one-on-one on a temporary basis, you will also help relieve the burden of overcrowding that every rescue and shelter bears. It is often the policy of a breed rescue that the foster family gets the right to adopt a dog they are fostering before the group considers any other applicant. You will garner the experience of what it's like to have the real thing, and you can gauge firsthand whether this breed is truly right for you. Rescue clubs will generally cover all food and medical expenses for the foster dog. Of course, once you adopt, the kibble's on you.

☻ If you have always loved this breed, but you are not in a position to own one at the present time, you can send in a donation and designate the money either for that rescue in general or for a particular dog. Many groups set up specific accounts to defray the costs of an expensive operation or disease treatment for one animal, and the website will feature her photo and story and keep you apprised of her progress. Once you are ready to fill out an application, it doesn't hurt your chances for your group of choice to be aware that you have been a financial supporter, however small or large, of their efforts.

☻ Find out when that breed rescue is having a "dog event," and go. People will bring their pets and talk dog for hours while getting acquainted. You will be able to easily get your petting fix and make new friends. I have never met a nicer group of people than those leashed to their favorite furballs. Hint: Halloween is the perfect time to see to what lengths humans will go to humiliate themselves and their dogs. Every year, the animal outfits get more outrageous and entertaining. Easter comes in a close second, but I would opt for October 31st as my favorite pet holiday.

☺ Click on the memorial page that most rescue websites carry. Allow the tears to well up while reading the tributes to these fallen but not forgotten angels. Note the various ages of the dogs who have died. You can easily find out the average life span of the breed you prefer by consulting any of a number of reference books or AKC statistics. You will get a better idea, however, from a rescue page.

It is a theory of mine, completely scientifically groundless, that adopted pets live longer lives on average. Doggedly sought after, heralded as heroes upon arrival home, these pooches are indulged to the max. They are on heartworm preventative, flea and tick preventative, have a standing appointment at the groomer, consume custom blended eats and play with a mountain of toys. You will find them stealing the limelight in the center of the family Christmas photos; occasionally fulfilling the duty of "flower dog" at a wedding; eating scrumptious liver cakes on their birthdays, doggie buddies in attendance, party hats pointing in all directions. If any animal has the best chance of living to a very ripe old age, it's the adopted dog.

SCOTTISH TERRIER

PAWS DOWN		PAWS UP	
Scott(y)	Mac	Brewster	Paisley
Angus	Morgan	Scooter	Flower
Duncan	Bonnie	Spanky	Kayne
McKenzie	Laddie	Pippin	Sunny

Isabelle

Priscilla

www.NorthTexasScottieRescue.com

www.ScottishTerrierRescue.org

www.ScottieKingdom.com

YORKSHIRE TERRIER

PAWS DOWN		PAWS UP	
New Yorkie	Bitsy	NikNak	Tornado
Button	Teeny	Mystery	Mallory
Killer	Terry	Kellee	Topaz
Teacup	Penny	Marvel	Lobo

Teddy

Savannah

www.YorkshireTerrierRescue.com

www.YorkieRescueMe.com

www.SOSDogs.org

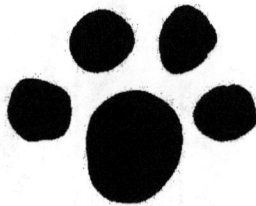

18

Hope Springs Eternal

There is one rescue experience I will never forget. It took six months to rehabilitate this little female, and a major portion of the group's resources at that time. But she is so worth it.

Every rescue group has at least one dog that serves as a symbol of their commitment to saving animals. When any group sets up a table at a fair or pet expo or other event, there will most likely be an easel displaying "before" and "after" photos of a particularly extreme case of neglect that resolved happily. "Hope" is one of those.

At present, "Hope" is joyfully residing with her forever family. But my first meeting with her was anything but joyful.

"Hope" was a dog estimated to be about nine months old who had been left in front of the **Ormond Beach, Florida**

Humane Society. Thank goodness the criminals left her there instead of merely tossing her onto the side of the road, although we presume, since "Hope" was in such bad shape, they didn't have the courage to bring her inside to surrender her. Because of her debilitating condition, our group was told that she had to be picked up in 24 hours or she would be euthanized. The shelter workers did not want to have her linger and suffer.

Within a few hours, Barbara, a **Buddies thru Bullies** volunteer, arrived on the scene. It was her task to take the dog and transport her to Orlando, where "Hope" would be transferred to yet another waiting vehicle that would continue her journey to rehab. At the Orlando meeting point, Barbara waited in her car, weeping. She had never seen a dog in such bad shape.

As Toby pulled into the parking lot, alarm gripped her. Why was Barbara crying? Had the young dog perished during the first leg of the trip? Did the pup somehow get loose and take off, nowhere to be found?

Barbara whispered that she had never encountered a dog victimized by such horrible neglect. With puffy, tear-streaked face and trembling arms, she tenderly gathered up the little bundle, and relinquished "Hope" to Toby.

There was an acute stench that permeated the air. "Hope" was hairless, except for a white tuft sprouting between her ears. She was covered with bloody, raw skin, the result of what would shortly be diagnosed as severe demodectic mange. Her skin was so thin that the blanket she was wrapped in had begun to stick to her.

Only days before, I had lost one of the great dogs of my heart, a giant, out-of-standard Bulldog that I had adopted when I first applied to be a member of my group. "Yankel" was a 90-pound, headstrong, 9-year-old sweetie who had been found wandering on the side of a highway. He had weighed 45 pounds when first picked up, and was nearly dead. But his will to live was stronger than any other dog I have seen. Richie and I adored him from the get-go, and "Yankel" shared our home (or maybe we shared "Yankel's" home) for three wonderful years.

I was grief-stricken when "Yankel" went to the Rainbow Bridge (a euphemism for the gates of heaven which every rescuer is familiar with and which is discussed in the next chapter). I felt an urgent need to take care of another dog, and when Toby informed me that "Hope" was on her way, I knew that pup was the answer to my prayer.

After a thorough examination by one of our vets, it was decided that the typical dip that mange-afflicted dogs usually get would be too toxic for "Hope" to endure. The chemicals would seep through her fragile skin and possibly kill her. Instead, she would get a daily dose of liquid Ivermectin squirted into her mouth – an activity reminiscent of the "pilling the cat" adventure.

103

In addition, she got oral antibiotics three times a day (thank goodness for peanut butter), and twice-daily medicated baths, followed by an application of a special lotion designed to speed healing and promote hair growth. The ailing pup's master suite consisted of a crate about twice the size of one that would ordinarily be appropriate for her, completely padded on all sides (I never liked that overstuffed quilt I got as a bridal shower gift anyway). Like cloth bumpers in a crib, this covering would prevent her from losing precious regenerating skin if she were to rub against the hard bars of her "apartment."

"Hope" was allowed to play in the backyard, but only for very limited periods. To avoid the danger of exposure to the harsh sun, I got her an oversized red and white striped doggie T-shirt which she reluctantly wore. The shirt became stained with the fluids oozing from her skin daily, so I invested in two tops, laundering one while "Hope" sported the other.

Within a few months, we discovered that this feisty little Bullie was mostly white with a few liver-colored spots. Nearly all her fur had grown back, and she was eating like a pig. "Hope" began to fill out rapidly, until she looked like a hairy little Hummer.

She had progressed so steadily and strongly that after six months, she was pronounced fit for adoption. When I manned a rescue table set up in PetSmart for **Buddies thru Bullies** at that time, I took "Hope" with me for her debut to the world. She greeted each and every passerby with a furious wag of her little butt, and I realized that she was ready for her forever family.

Some months after "Hope" was adopted, I received a picture of her which we use on our easel at various events as the "after" photo. No one would ever be able to connect that robust, stocky white Bulldog in the picture with the pathetic bundle of infected skin and bones in the "before" shot. Suffice it to say that each rescue group has many "Hope" stories of its own, and will quickly point to the joyous "after" photos as evidence of the fulfillment of its rewarding mission.

19

A Fond Farewell

Dog lover though you are, you may not be aware of the Rainbow Bridge. This is a lovely piece, author unknown, written to bring a bit of solace to the grieving pet owner. As with everything else, there is indeed a website, in fact, several of them, that feature the Rainbow Bridge story. It does have some minor variations in wording from site to site, but the sentiments are exactly the same:

"Just this side of heaven is a place called Rainbow Bridge. When an animal dies that has been especially close to someone here, that pet goes to Rainbow Bridge.

"There are meadows and hills for all of our special friends so they can run and play together. There is plenty of food, water and sunshine, and our friends are warm and comfortable.

"All the animals who had been ill and old are restored to health and vigor. Those who were hurt or maimed are made whole and strong again, just as we remember them in our dreams of days and times gone by. The animals are happy and content, except for one thing: they each miss someone very special to them, who had to be left behind.

"They all run and play together, but the day comes when one of their number suddenly stops and looks into the distance. His bright eyes are intent. His eager body quivers. Suddenly, he begins to run from the group, flying over the green grass, his legs carrying him faster and faster.

"You have been spotted, and when you and your special friend finally meet, you cling together in joyous reunion, never to be parted again. The happy kisses rain upon your face. Your hands again caress the beloved head, and you look once more into the trusting eyes of your pet, so long gone from your life but never absent from your heart.

"Then you cross the Rainbow Bridge into heaven together... "

I'm a sucker for a sad or poignant story. I cried when Bambi's mother got shot (I own a copy of the movie, and *every* time I watch it, I cry when Bambi's mother gets shot). But the Rainbow Bridge story cleans me right out of tissues.

There are a few variations, if you will, of the Rainbow Bridge.

108

After the tragedy of 9/11, a very special Bridge adaptation made its way across the internet. In this version, pets who had been abandoned at shelters and who had died without being adopted, lined up by the Rainbow Bridge to greet each one of those who had perished that horrific day, and to accompany the victims across, united in spirit.

The Rainbow Bridge story that hits me right in my rescue heart is the one that follows, and I dedicate this to all my devoted buddies whose passion for this work has made the world a brighter place:

"Unlike most days at Rainbow Bridge, this day dawned cold and gray, as damp and dismal as could be imagined. All of the recent arrivals had no idea what to think, as they had never experienced a day like this before.

"But the animals who had been waiting for their beloved people for some time knew exactly what was going on and started to gather at the pathway leading to the Bridge to watch.

"It wasn't long before an elderly animal came into view, head hung low and tail dragging. The other animals, the ones who had been there for a while, knew what his story was right away, for they had seen this happen far too often.

"He approached slowly, obviously in great emotional pain but with no sign of injury or illness. Unlike all of the other animals waiting at the Bridge, this one had not been restored to youth and made vigorous again. As he trudged toward the Bridge, he saw all of the other animals watching him. He knew he was out of place here, and the sooner he could cross over, the better.

"Unfortunately, as he approached the Bridge, his way was barred by the appearance of an angel, who apologized, but told him that he would not be able to pass. Only those animals who were with their people could pass over the Rainbow Bridge. With no place else to turn to, the elderly creature slowly made his way toward the fields near the Bridge and saw a group of animals like himself, also aged and frail. They weren't playing, rather simply lying on the grass, forlornly staring out at the pathway leading to the Bridge. So he took his place among them, watching the pathway, and waiting.

"One of the new arrivals at the Bridge didn't understand what he had just witnessed, and he asked one of the animals that had been there for awhile to explain.

"'You see,' the more experienced one said, 'that poor animal was a rescue. He was turned in to rescue just as you see him now, older, with his fur graying and his eyes clouding. He was never adopted, and so passed on with only the love of his rescuer to comfort him as he left his earthly existence.

"'Because he had no family to give his love to, there will be no one to escort him across the Bridge.'

"The first animal thought about this for a minute, and then asked, 'So what will happen to him now?' As he was about to receive his answer, the clouds parted and the gloom began to lift.

"Approaching the Bridge could be seen a single person, and among the old rescue animals, the whole group was suddenly bathed in a golden light. They were young and vibrant again, just as they had been in the prime of life.

"'Watch this,' whispered the second animal. A group of pets from those waiting for their loved ones lined both sides of the pathway and bowed deeply as the person neared. To each lowered head, the person offered a gentle pat or a scratch behind the ears.

"The newly restored animals fell into line behind her and followed her toward the Bridge. They all crossed the Bridge together.

"'What happened?' asked the first pet.

"'That was a rescuer. The animals you saw bowing in respect were those who found new homes because of her work. They will cross when their new owners arrive. Those you saw restored were those who never found homes.

"'When a rescuer arrives at the Bridge, they are allowed to

perform one final act of rescue. They are allowed to escort those animals they couldn't place on earth, across the Rainbow Bridge.'

"'I think I like rescuers,' said the first animal.

"'Yes,' was the reply. 'So does God.'"

THE END

.